Cromwell Milton Collins Carson

Cantos CLIII-CLXIV and Cantos CLXXXII-CXCVII

from *Yrland Regained CENTRAL CANTOS*

by

KEVIN KIELY

Contents

Cromwell Milton CANTOS

CLIII

'three events in our history, which may be regarded as touch-
stones [...]
an English Whig who asserts the reality of the popish
plot; an Yrish Catholic who denies the massacre of 1641;
and a Scotch Jacobite who maintains the innocence of
Queen Mary, must be considered as men beyond the reach
of argument or reason, and must be left to their
own prejudices'
—David 'Bigot' Hume *Enquiry Concerning Human
Understanding* (1748)

'it has become a Proverb in England, to call a dull
Unthinking Fellow, a Man of an Yrish Understanding'
—George Story *Continuation of the Impartial History* (1693)

London's 'official history' from Story & 'Tory-Scot' Hume
          XVI-XVII century varieties propagandist rhetoric

Treise leat, a Chromuil,/A rígh chroinic na sculóg
As red linn fuaramuir suaimhnios,/Mil, eachtar agus onóir
—Séafra Ó Donnchadha
more power to your elbow Cromwell/old monarch of ancient
chronicle
your reign was all peace, honey, cream and honours bestowed on us

'we came, by the assistance of G-d, to hold forth and maintain the
lustre and glory of English liberty in a nation (Yrland) where we
have an undoubted right to do it'

Oliver *wartface* Cromwell

                                     terminal 'friend' of Yrland
Ringsend's slaughtered sky mirrors what they execute

ships docking, sounds of Ormond's cannons, Ss

Brendan Kennelly (XX century) accosted on O'Connell Bridge
whoi did you write
about Cromwell cut-throat butcher Brit? demanded of the
Kerryman.

Smedley HP Food Factory (1974) strawberries, potatoes, carrots,
peas & pies
Ely cathedral 'smoking' cannabis (Moroccan)
in a tin pipe & the sign *Keep off the Grass*

near Cromwell's house, National Trust thatch
walls, black planks white-wash redolent of pitch, fire & swords
Nolly Crommy nuclear on Yrish and his Cambridgshire
accent: *you ol-royt*
yeh arr-UUU
winter Birmingham Pub deaths, IRA bombs
Tabloid headline: *BASTARDS*
factory canteen Brits menacing eyes on the Yrish
                BMPs interviews 'investigating' Sundays' clock-in
cards of 'Paddies'
                            & Mick Hayes hastily out of Britain
Conlons rounded up like Allen, Larkin & O'Brien

Pamela *Lemon Crepe & Coffee*
 Dawson Street (2016)
re-iterated
'Why' amidst small talk

Kennelly's Olly Nolly Cromby 'foepal […] a whack on the jaw
    on O'Connell Bridge' for rhyming the dictator on TV

& Kennelly bought a vagrant woman coffee
said goodbye: *Mind yourself now, try and keep*
your knickers on

                  O'Neills Suffolk Street (1976)
Kennelly a *Tayto* bag-bomb

                on the counter & his flat hand
                'you get more crisps this way'
                'all Yrishmen crucified between
                good woman/bad woman'
                bean fionn sí and her Morrigan

Cromwell's sooty warts on eyelids, man-witch proud
London killer James Bible in saddle bags

towards Papists 'cloven footed' & 'with tails'
'had tails nearly a quarter of a yard long; 40 soldiers
    […] testified the same on their oaths'

'a company of poisonous papish ceremonies'
                Nash *Hudibras*
motto on Crummy's keepsake handkerchief *Pax Quaeritur Bello*
peace be sought through war

Cromwell, pseud of Cambridgeshire
university drop-out, Paisley's counterfeit PhD

gets into politics, into army, covers ALL Saxon-Brit politicos

cast list, bleary eyes dreary moon faces
Heavy Metal Ozzie Ozbourne *Black Sabbath* lookalike

Crummy weds into money with Elizabeth Bourchier
 you hear Norman-Saxon
they're in the 'dowry house' Ely with kids in shoes made by slaves

he's in Westminster, usual locations: Whitehall & Palaces
Crummy governor of Ely, eyes set on the crown
Crummy gathers gent-snobs & their
diehard
monarch pomp & circumstance, pretence to pull all down
to commoners: Civil War, Beheaded King on his CV

before the Irish Tour

CLIV

transition of many, thank you
Iowa City's river, twisting in honey laden flow
sun's furnace & sits on the grass

Gary Snyder talks of ploughing thru *Paradise Lost* in Piute Creek
    'God created Adam, Eve and Satan'

& Marianne Backlén buddhist
      'hashish & joss sticks prolong lovemaking'

      visionary hemp & shadows opening dimensions

      plasma spirit startles, glistening eyes pale-torches
            face-sized soap bubble

Satan and Oliver become Gothic Stan and Olly
'I got a poem out of yr Milton,' he points
quoting 'O hell what do mine eyes with grief behold'

Yrish hell, post-Kinsale, post-Flight of 'Earls'
      never were Yrish earls, says Pamela Yrland
         'earls' London class-thing, Tory racism 'no riff-raff'
          —anyway 1607 ninety of the O'Neill-O'Donnell clans
            last night in Sweeney-Doe's castle
              had hatched Gunpowder Plot
        for Westminster, Yrish bombing London per usualü

poets' grief, spirit women at weirs
hill forts, by streams by boulders

'oft' overhung with willows

                                        beán fíonn sí rising

misogynist Milton misses Moses & Girl Friday boating
on the Nile
delicious fruit of God
sensuality, sweat and fluid blissful, body's vineyard flowing rivers
intoxicants consensual beatitude
                        Genesis windows the flimsy underwear
                              touch of thistledown on genitalia
                                        genitalia flora, fauna

all trees are Eden
knowledge, benediction nature's beatitude
Milton's Eden is the cold English garden
fenced off, military machinery oiled in blood
'love in fear the onely God'
                  'he first acquired the government of himself', Milt
says of Crummy
                        government of himself 'ahem' FFS
                        London is Westminster fear-en-
dowed populus

                        Naw, shouts Gary to the falling sun
                        river perfect lid of glass bronze

glimpse of *Hancher Auditorium*
poster [*Rhapsody in Blue* &]

          let's get music, Marianne with her bit-lip smile

He was not a man of blood says Edward Hyde
Oggsfordian, non-judiciously viciously praises Cromwell of

calloused blood,
the imposture of religious piety

Milton's subconscious model for Satan is

Cromwell, yes Milton & Marvell

in collective actions, words and condemnations

lower than three baboons

same hair length, same ears, but your teeth never as clean

no three baboons with such cruel faces & deeds

mass slaughters

Darwen stream, with blood of Scots inbrued (Milton)

& sniggering at a king you dispatched

not that Liffey other than cheered

royal spanielness, Charley I his biggest crime marrying a French
Papist

Nolly, Johnny and Andy racism was yr true faith,

puritanism yr propaganda pack of cards [...]

blood stains on yr bible like

England's war poppies

                              hanging on by a bunch of

plastic poppies

                       you owe those you slew for holding

stolen lands

                       hypocrites of the fallen, fallen
                       Westminster, Whitehall &

Fuckingham Palace

                       & Scotland swells yr headaches
1637 Stony Sunday *Book of Common Prayer*
antagonistic John Knox's *Book of Common Order*
where *Rex est Lex* refuted
William Laud, Archbish Canterbury 'confused' over Dissenters
Laud 1640 arrested, executed January 1645

Cromwell his New Model Army
 'go and fight the battles of the Lord'
enter Milton antiPresby, anti Voltaire's masterpiece *Candide*
                              anti, anti, anti […] Yrish
England blessed *by the favour and love of Heaven*

of course, Milton hurrays
Cromwell's *God for the liberty of his conscience*
             Paradise Lost not in print until Cromwell dead

        'the uprising in Yrland has greatly increased

        the malice of the puritans [...] it has

        universally disposed people to believe

        anything evil about the Catholics'

State Papers, Westminster 1641-43.

Thus 1641, John Thomas (brit prick) and John Pym
prime plea for killing

Westminster passes *Act for Adventurers*
11 February 1642

offering lands from potential pool

yea chunky acreage to any soldier who kills rebels

'most barbarously exquisite in tormenting the poore Protestants,
wheresoever they come, cutting off their private members, eares,
fingers, and hands, plucking out their eyes, boyling the heads of
little
children before their Mothers faces, and then ripping up their
mothers
bowels, stripping women naked, and standing by them naked [...]
Worse and worse news from Ireland (1641) Nathaniel Butter

'the massacre of Lady Barrymore and her family most inhu-
manely
murdered by the Rebels'

Protestant peers flee Dublin
print official propaganda & newsbooks
'false and palpably feigned overnight in English ale houses'

Crummy Cromwell (1649) all other newsbooks withdrawn, seized,
banned—

                    illegal printing at bond £300 on arrest—
                    London censorship on queue
                    Milton's reality Hell aka London

CLV

        Crummy's busy year, backdated to
1642 Owen Roe O'Neill arrives by Papal pressure
   on Spain to become commander
of Ulster armies

January-June 1643 Dublin
Ormond with Kilkenny Catholic Confererates

Dr Robert Maxwell rector Armagh captured/released by Rebels
        his 'witness' of 154,000 Prods massacred
    printed as *fact* by Westminster, 1643
            lies, lies, lies says beán fíonn sí
Wednesday's mercury makes it 200,000
(including Lady Barrymore?)
Britanicus conservative figure 100,000
'tying Ministers and their wives back to back, cruelly putting them
to death,
 and all this cruelty exercised on them, because they were Protes-
tants,
and yet these <u>unparaleld</u> Popish Rebels are by a Protestant King
called
subjects'
      Britanicus concludes 'Yrish are ungrateful subjects
of the king'
Britanicus proofreading troubles hence <u>unparaleld</u>
but upscales the figure (weeks later) 120,000 killed
prints *Rebellion in Irelande*

The spie writes 'savage, brutish, Yrish Kernes, whose wickednesse
 and irreligion, renders them altogether void of the common principles
of humanity'

'hear, hear' sayeth Westminster
Summer 1644 time for British justice!
Aulicus declares 'wash them to death from the blood
of the Prods that was upon them'

Owen Roe O'Neill at Benburb his army 5,000
massacre 3000 of the King's men
    & some of the king's horses

Kingdomes Weekly Intelligencer on Battle of Benburb 500-600 Brits fallen
Autumn 1647 O'Neill burns crops
around Pale forces an Yrish-welcoming famine
                on planters

Truce with Rebels August 1648
              Yrland is writing Charley's (Charles I) death
warrant

the Moderate headline 21 November 1648
'his Majestie himself was, and is the Capitoll Author,
Contriver, Abettor, and Mannager of all the blood-shed, massa-
cres,
and whatsoever ruins have befallen not only this Kingdom, but also
that of Yrland'

the Moderate (a Cromwell publication)
                & protoTory press-feed to 1998

London does zany king-trial and regicide
                two-part tragic/farce
a right Charlie before High Court, 26 January 1649
                        yea, king unravelled because of Yrland (lie)
beheaded for High Treason 30 January outside Whitehall
                            Milton among spectators 'straining
with his one good eye'
(weeks later) 6 March 1649 New Army ships sail for Yrland
Cromwell appoints himself, Herr Cromwell
Commander-in-chief & by himself in Westminster
fears Scottish disloyalty, more
than Yrland's papists 'pay-pests'
coz Charley has to lose his 'ead, he is er, Scotsman
Milton hastily publishes *The Tenure of Kings*
pickled propaganda
for Bloody Sundays, Mondays, Tuesdays, Wednesdays
Thursdays, Fridays, Saturdays 'revenge the blood of the many
 thousands that hath been spilt of their blood
by Commissions from the late King Charles' in Yrland
during 1641-1649
                —4 May 1649 *Mercurius*
Britannicus

government printing presses
        noisier than an army on the march
excess 6,000 pamphlets with anti-Irish material
circulate in England
not once, does name 'Charles I' appear in *The Tenure of Kings*
war is obedience to death-dealing rulebook
                Nolly Crummy salivates like hungry dog

'hated' by royalist Ussher of TCDublin Ussher anti-pape
        suck to Crummy, granted an audience
                coughing back ecclestiastical heresy
                    'divine love hierarchical'
fatis agimur, credite fatis fate leads us, believe it (lit)
burial of Ussher in Westminster Abbey Rome's envy, Ireland's
loss, and England's gain stony lines by Quarles hack poet
                    Ussher like Swift, f'ked out of London
Ussher's green hate swansong *Of the religion profeffed*
        by the Ancient Yrish rants about O'Sullivan Beare
Ussh lines of hate for O'Neills, O'Donnells
              Yrish war genius grows 'Regained'

Ussher's 'greatest howler' claims God creates the world
        on October 22, 4004 BC: you saxon whorson bore-slob
                fk off back to London

Milt peddles the 154,000 massacre LIE
        purveyes absurdity of Charles I
Eikonoklastes XII 'no understanding man could longer
        doubt who was author or instigator of that Rebellion'
(Charley 2 green-shirts) what BS, Charley claims hierarchy
              Westminster's ghoul gang are hidden
        Hierarchy, Charles writes *Eikon Basiliké*
'suffer those men long to prosper in their Babel, who built it
        with bones, and cement it with the blood of kings'
            yea, they'll top you for your eloquence

CLVI

& (*Searlas*) Charles One the court case (comedy central)
oblong Westminster Hall, see his
coffin pined primed athwart palace of Westminster
his royal silk stockings cause laughter
drops his royal cane, silver knob rolls off
no one picks it up, king retrieves his own knob and cane
          no applause
    king bends, scrapes his knob off floor
Cromwell raves to Sidney *i tell you, we will cut off*
his head with the crown upon it

Charles I shaggy dog story, head-chopping their own
kinkque of Hinkland forenenst Whitehall
Charlie Two Shirts, well 'twas January 20, 1649
they slice the twerp's head from his neck and shoulders
'the gaudy name of Majesty' *Eikonoklastes*
ole Axeman commeth, creaking like rusty hinges
fie foh and fum, I smell the blood of a British man
shouts Cromwell for what is a king? 'em, ordinary bloke poncing
about
with stagy crooked crown
    clown's clothes
Milton condemns kingship except for *King Cromwell*
monarchy not divine thus 'people who gave themselves a king'
occult lieth not never, dixit Mister Yeats's *Vision*
                    of actions replete on earth
final cue ball sound, his doomed knob rolling
along wooden tiles, ripped out from Yrland
    war slaughter of hackings, jaggings

London executions by this year
anti-climax, crowd find it hard
to source ale and wenches plying their trade
Charles dull theatre plays no ordinary prisoner
with divine right (ended with *Magna Carta*)
& no plea to their 'corrupt' (never!) court
king above the Law, powerless to kill a king

>   but they 'ave the

hold-all *Magna Corrupta*
long gone, Crummy bull whistles: Charley public enemy
warrant signed as London does, thus Cromwell
sneers as proto-loyalist
failed pageantry, false trial

justice roared by the guards before proceedings close
>   'Justice and Execution'

as if final act is 'anything new' either side of Thames
condemned man's (not king's) speech 'taxes' everyone's patience
as with speeches of Edward II, Richard II, Mary Queen of Scots
yea, Richard II as per Holinshed's tight lipped chronicles
'felled with a stroke of a poleaxe'
Holinshed afeared for his head (London censorship)
'felled' by one axe stroke
Sir Piers of Exton with Saxon sentimentality
pretends the murderer weeps after the event
>   Crummy with a wet handkerchief
>   over Charles I (never!)

London graffiti:
Queen Bess orders one Bloody Mary:
her sister's head

CLVII

head chop delay, accommodate anti
Accession Act *Abolition of Monarchy Act*
Westminster *makes it up as it goes along*
Magna Carta fits any state legal situation—
wanted: one head of King
Charley I in two-Shirts, last day of January
last indeed, friend Tom Herbert asks to be excused
doesn't want to hear chopping, or thud
                'tho-od'
head not as heavy as you'd think, falling off
                      like Brit-clunk-accent
Andrew Marvel among the crowd
kept at bay by Cromwell's *New Army* on Parade
            'New' is propaganda: brigands/underlings,
proto Black & Tans
               (usual beggared psycho thugs)
               open secret of Westminster
               national poverty regulator, welfare
regulator
               HM as royal summons

        English armies 'job, uniform, weapons training
              in exchange for poverty'
true in Crummy's day as 35-year war Yrland

              few politicians took it on the chin from
              Irish Republicans, mainly Brit-troops
              lads joined to see the world of
              South Armagh, South Down,

South Tyrone
                    Bandit Country for leprechaun Óglaighí
                              off duty in Drogheda & Dundalk
                                        Safe South Houses & Pubs:
32 County Selection

                    B&Bs, G&BKs (gun & bomb kits)

                              boozing to kill Brits
                              pay back Crummy's hell fire

& further propaganda from the mess hall

not a chance, Marvell skunk-coward stays away on the day
loyal to Adolf von Hitler-Cromwell who also stays away
so king Wally Chally makes pathetic speech about liberty and
freedom for people of England [...]
                                        yes, 'freedom!'
                    whereas in Yrland:
And leave us in our utmost need to Cromwell's cruel blow
Sheep without a shepherd when the snow shuts out the sky—

Davis (of poets) national laments works green bile
                    pushes to 'Regained'

& the poisoning of Eoghan Rua O'Neill
        & Martin McGuiness (2017) not mainstream news yet
                    London ever vengeful

                    belches forth a cow-faced dyspeptic scug
                              vile death manufacturing Crummy

'these bloody Papists [...] cruelties and tortures exceeding all
parallel, unheard of among Pagans, Turks, or Barbarians, except

you would enter into the confines of Hell itself'

—James Cranford

The Teares of Ireland (1642)

pamphlets support
3,000 'survivors' sworn testimonies from 1641-9 war
'started by rebels' (as usual) Sir Phelim O'Neill and continued by
Owen Roe O'Neill

Milton's hackwork *Against the Yrish rebels* (1649)
author of *Paradise Lost* 'those Yrish barbarians' 'mortal en-
emies' 'merciless'
places his name to conjecture
massacre more than 200,000 prod settlers, according to Milt
       who never set foot in Yrland (changing estimates)

William Hickman 10 February 1649:
'God hath marked out that people (Yrish) for destruction'

he-aw, he-aw

August 15, 1649 Cromwell heaves in sight of Ringsend, Dublin
throat belches seasickness

snot flem with stale bread
hates travel by sea, vomits his guts up
white faced as corpse, creator of corpses
       'tummy, where's my mummy?'
campfires crackle wood from Dublin mountains

buys his food from 'stinking papists' Gaelic words in their speech
'English nobleman' promises genocide
spits out boiled potato into goat's milk
bainne gabhair ná gleanta a Mhaistír
he's gone ashy pet Kate in bad moods

Psalms shouted out by Stephen Jerome
& Hugh Peters wearing stove pipe hats with buckles
beards dripping saliva, dirt marked faces, muddy hands
    'soldiers hear me afore you turn in for sleep
cursed be he that maketh not the sword stark drunk with Yrish
blood [...]
maketh them in heaps on heaps [...] let not that eye look for pity,
nor hand be
spared [...] let him be cursed that curseth them not bitterly'
—Nathaniel Ward London 1647 *Pamphlet*

        well said Nat, you Brit-gnat thug
      Milton's theology bookish nil dimensions
   reality is State and church (controlled by Westminster)
        Milt for hatred above poetry
        The female bee that feeds her

husband drone

        Deliciously, and builds her waxen

cells

        With honey stored
       Milt preaches genocide 'to leave this para-
dise, but shalt possess
A paradise within thee, happier far.'
        Cromwell's Yrland his vision of failure & England's

CLVIII

Crummy's men in Dublin
polish sharpen swords with rags
                kneel in worship to cannons & guns
                                trim instruments for efficient death

pray for heaps of slashed leaking corpses

Cromwell (Crummy) with Charles I beheaded January
England thru Civil War previous year

Mao-Cromwell Tse-Tung *preserve one's forces, annihilate the
enemy*
[...] avoid passive inflexible methods

Sun Tzu's wartime policy *moral influence*
force people in accord with superiors
                perfect national propaganda, have yr war and eat it
war is based on deception Sun Tzu tells
        war never accidental
planned like roads, hospitals, sewers, prostitutes, wages

noise of war is national war music

cannons do not silence seagulls, Ringsend cattle butchered
soldiers wait for roasted beasts & to rape Yrish peasants
                thrust of erect member, thrust of sword

Crummy's sidekick Ireton preening Parliamentarian Troops
infantry, horse soldiers amidst dung hills
                                Ringsend icy winds

loathsome Papist natives
Papist women breeding Papes
litters of them
drown 'em in Yrish Sea
clear island to forests, rivers, lakes, mountains, crop fields,
cattle, sheep
birds & fishes for Crummy's God-fearing folk

useful Ysland, annexed were it not for Yrish vermin
and their priestlings
      and how Crummy's gang speak of killing
women like rabbits
victory is the object of war. If this is long delayed
weapons are 'blunted'
and morale depressed—Sun Tzu

Crummy's expedition delays, military practice (in between)
beyond Drogheda looms Ulster he treads not there
horizon & mountains, pine conifer ridges
  Kerne fortresses

Drogheda hated as in 35 year, Six County War
in real narrative
  Crummy gets ill
yea, no-king bum, sick to Hell
    in papist curses
Ysland's hidden weaponry
    London knows nought of
& food 'sold' to invading armies
  spells, poisoned water
medieval sorcery, mosquitos
      insects infected, thorn pricks

CLIX

along a plain, weary, follows the Boyne
     wary, keeping the hated Yrish sea in sight
               cowards look back to Dublin
                     (epic narrative, eh?)
                          unnerving mountains, South Ulster
                               horizons maddening
                                    mountains stack up

vastnesses fastnesses
to sink the heart

                               Yrland unconquerable?
                               unmentionable, perturbs him
                          other illnesses, guts in damp climes

stomach cannonading

                          weak limbs, sweat like vinegar
pallor of sour milk
Yrland begins his vomiting
                     diarrhoeia, fevers, body cramps malarial
symptoms, hate fuses his

frame into more murders

                               & Yrland slashes back
                               gives his grave journey

west bank castellated town, double-tower gateways Drogheda

subdue the enemy without fighting is perfection in war
—Sun Tzu
Crummy sends horsemen demanding surrender
'we shall grant quarter'
worst policy: attack towns and cities—Sun Tzu

Arthur Aston's 2,000 defend Drogheda
'No Surrender' September 10, 1649

next day artillery, walls breached with cannonballs, hell of a to-do
12,000 English roundheads

> stink of gunpowder, smoke
> weapons clang-a-lang

trying to breach Duleek Gate, Boyne River west bank

foot soldiers over broken wall
Aston beaten to death with his wooden leg, mocked
didn't run him through like a soldier
musket fire, swords for butchery
bloodied flow amassing bubbling
flowering in crimson, fading colour of eyes
egg white grey, Yrish speaking not English—
> Papists to Hell

Gaelic language must be stopped, language to kill
swords smell of kill
wounded/dying noisy agony, pike them into silence
cloven footed with tails, spare no one, children
chop heads, squealing babes
blood from necks emptying, emptying
 on straw, on wood, on mud

soon time for food, whole town to loot
frantic search for hiding females

                              entrails hacked flesh, limbs broken, proud
days's work

tunics armour stained, soldiers laugh at last
wink at comrades, blood smattered like Charles I—
 stable horses in papist churches (always)

CLX

& after dusk a Papist Church
hides ladies of the town, some
in their Sunday best, fear-stricken tear-stained children

swing of slashing swords, warm blood on pews
                              drops of papist wine
                                        dead corpse faces cut

We come by the assistance of God to hold forth and maintain the lustre
and glory of English liberty in a nation where we have an un-
doubted
right to it
Cromwell speaks with DUP Pais-Nazi-ley face

& how they cheer, 'soldiers well ye do by me'

                    in action karma, in rough-hewn divinity
Cromwell's genocide Drogheda 11 September
given no newsbook status
'first eminent action'
'Depositions' in John Dod's *Perfect diurnall* news-sheet
Yrish cannibals

                    Crummy 'learns' a lot in Yrland:
                         England's Yrish fate
                              regicine needs of London—
                                   takes his head

posthumously

> London kings inadvertently 'help' Yrland
> conquest two-way flow
> real history

Lord Louis's morning boat ride to Hell
1979
'heard' among echoes

> loudly in Drogheda & Wexford
> being 330 years after Crummy

revenge rapid as rivers
whirlpools froth against rocks

> *beán fíonn sí* aggrieved, demands
> green phoenixes rise from

executed green phoenixes

CLXI

Crumy's profile is Satan & hells angles the New Army
                    in Drogheda—
the state is 'God'=Cromwell
Milton schizoid, implies God is Charles I
                                    & Adam to be executed
outside Eden
'There they take their fill of love and love's disport/Took
largely, of their mutual Guilt the seal' (IX)
                    Restoration of evil
not God, not woman, not life
Milt writes hate learns regicide mania
        Westminster, works for government
'For never can true reconcilement grow/where sounds
 of deadly hate/Have pierced so deep' (IV)
thus Yrland's history glowers at London

Paradise Lost Milton prays to Satan ü
musical lines in hate breeding hate
 Milt waits & outs Crummy dressed as Satan in print
        BUT 'after' Crummy's death

'So farewell hope, and with hope farewell fear, farewell
remorse! All good/To me is lost; Evil, be thou my good' (IV)
thus Drogheda, Wexford

Adam and Eve post-Cromwellian Londoners:
'He for God only, she for God in him' (IV)
                                Milt is England's misogyny

'Disturbances on earth through female snares, and strait
 conjunction with this sex' (IX)
                                        Milt is woman-jailer
Milt 'Spaniel Man' sonorous genius bigot collaborator
accessory to Yrish genocide on Westminster payroll

                    weak homiliac theology, shiny chestnuts
                            never plucks any delicious fruit—
panto Lucifer morphs to Satan
                    Milton's pallid "Hymn to Cromwell"

Milt weak nagging, no-conscience
if God is perfect, he creates an Angel that falls
                    is of no interest to Milt's inferno
                            failed theological content

'evil' ultimately desired, sanctioned by Satan
        Dell superhero demonic ruler of Gotham
                    Milton's true love Cromwell-Satan

'Satan, whom now transcendent glory rais'd above his
 fellows with Monarchal pride' […]
'Conscious of highest worth'
Cromwell's profile—
primogenitor Tory kills
snarling demogogue Tory tyrants
                    ancestors Churchill, Thatcher, Major, Blair,
Cameron, May, Johnston
                                    (all born in Nazireth, London)

                    Milt finds war is Heaven
                    thus, naturally war on earth
                    Honoré Benet's 'wars

existed first in Heaven'

English Premier League: Paradise 0 Hell 1

Milt's *Paradise Regained*
                              pedestrian, disinterested biblical precis
Jesus sleeps under a juniper tree
                              awakens to supper prepared by
demoted angels
                              (*Paradise Lost* 'Hell' is London)
alive thou art Milton in satanic imaginings
     on wings of stagey stage play
'set a woman in his eye and in his walk'
               amidst rawmeish theology
peccavi 'hammering out of our own hearts, as it were
out of flint, the seeds and sparkles of new misery
 to ourselves, till all were a blaze again'
Milt apes his 'chief of men'
poison hateful adjectives

'the last means to avoid popery, is to amend our lives'
                    'a pontifical despotism decked out under the
pretence of religion'
                    Gary Snyder buys zilsch of this philosophy
                              on Iowa River, or any river

Miltonic linguistics majestic
corseted laced governmental pomp

via Cromwell's *Englishe Reichland*
                    Milton arts council poet at base,
                         at best real poet within nazzydom
                              thrown off Parnassus for toryism
                              knows Empire's evil enacts

against green Ysland Eden

free fruit, free love

beán fíonn sí *cailín Aoife*

agus a fear Paddy Adams

& Mr Sam Beckett's

'beastly bigot Milton!'

John Milton bought state-

funded poet

muzzled to scribble propa-

ganda, ancestor Joe Goebbels

CLXII

Cromwell sees half-moon as papist mitre
9/11 is 11/9 County Louth (*Lugh Lamh Fhada*)

Twin Towns Slaughter Festival *Cromwell Day* Drogheda
& Dundalk

& south to Wexford bleeds Emerald Eden
swords, instruments of abattoir
brimming pools of Papists along Drogheda's
 Stockwell Street
Duleek Street, St Peter's Church vibrates in blowback
                         genocide

beán fíonn sí visits Cromwell's soldiers
slaughtered in Clonmel
by Eoghan Roe O'Neill's army

Yrish few escape, flee Twin Towns, tell wide-eyed
and are heard

failing to capture Clonmel where hundreds of Cromwell's
butchers
WERE slashed by O'Neill's army who lured them with promises
of
surrender, coaxed the brits through archway and there released a
Saxon
sleet of blood

do it again Clonmel, gore the butchers' their imperialist gore eternally, anniversary of Crummy's exhumation

cut out Saxon tongues before their eyes
hear muffled curses choking on their tongues

Roy Foster sold to twentieth century Oxford,
Lying, that Cromwell
'betrays an uncharacteristically uneasy tone' on
Yrish wars. Tosh on payroll
                    Crummy weeps over Drogheda & Wexford
                            like Jesus over Jerusalem?
papists, wild Yrish
give those papists torture, sword and gibbet, requires maximum

tracts & *news books* Regicidal chaos

Charles' bleeding dumb-head

in Whitehall, Cromwell's puppet trial by
committee

& lackey English poets: Marvell's cruel lines
and now the Yrish are ashamed
to see themselves in one year tamed

Cromwell 9 months in total in Yrland
gang of Thugs offer him crown of England
King Olly Wally Wan

April 1657 like Shakespeare's *Richard II*
Crum toys with royal offer'!

he that kills a king can be king for farce
      King Farce Face Nth
his tyrant wits hold all minions in commons
in common, London snob-lies about difference
fears the seal of regicide
take his crown and head off
to be crowned May 7 but rumblings
among House of Commons
and Crum refuses to be resident king
and IS despot dictator

  ego poeta buries Ussher

                        'graal' affectation, Glastonbury myth
                        Arimathea proto-Tory vulgar tomb
bestower

                        Ussher attends execution Charles I
                        watches from Lady Peterborough's
house, an anti-regicide

                        coward among tea-cups, woodworm
tennis rackets
yes you bigot, Jacobi Usserii

                        fledgling proser 'power communi-
cated by God to

                        the prince' you tell 'em posthumously
                  dedicated to Charles II by yr estate keeper
good man Ussher: yourself
                        had it both ways loyalist and TCD whisperer—
sham theologian 'God created the world' on October 22, 4004 BC
                  Greenwich Mean Time, you wacko

CLXIII

time slowly brings swift karma

Charles II's mistresses, plus Frances Stewart model
for Britannia coins with helmet and trident
restoration post-Puritan party scenes
John Wilmot, earl of Rochester poet:
                                different to Milt's mighty
untheological line
Much wine had passed with grave discourse
Of who fucks whom and who does worse [...]

by dildoes worn as regal crowns
& courtiers wearing eiderdowns
& London smiles in blood red gowns

That pattern of virtue, Her Grace of Cleve-land
Has swallowed more pricks than the ocean has sand

& the Great Fire started in Westminster, blamed on Papists [...]
England religiously dissensioned, diverse beliefs and sects [...]
Presbyterian Scots presumed 'defeated' by Cromwell [...]

Marvell lives to see Cromwell defamed
by Charles II
wobbly crown, hangovers and Chas II orders exhumation

lo and behold corpse-hung, corpse-beheaded
Cromwell as showcase revenge *explicitus ad hoc*
'dig up what remains of the fucker!'

Charles II (1660) demands Cromwell, Ireton & Bradshaw
exhumed, no less & lackey Marvell edits his
Odes to Cromwell

                makes them 'Charley II friendly'

Charles II has John Cook arrested in Yrland, Cook prosecuted
his Dad (Charley I) in the bogus Cromwell-cooked up treason
trial hosted by Whitehall cheers
(england's history IS cartoon narrative)
Cook beheaded on same spot, block draped in black, falls
the axe, more Saxon blood flows—

                more power to yr elbow

Axeman, many's a citizen

                in *Dublin-sur-Liffey* who'd

help you for free

                with shamrock on their hats

corpses of Cromwell, Ireton, Bradshaw dragged to Tyburn
(get off at Marble Arch Underground)
EIGHT blows to sever Cromwell's dead mutton rotten, dead head
    thence upon a spike outside Westminster Hall
until 1684 'Pongwell'
    london do good karma, eh?

pretty pretty sight on spike, hail 'cromwell crumble!'

where Cromwell's bits are buried is not known
                        clerical error/Westminster screw up
who fucking cares in Drogheda, Dundalk
            & Wexford

Cromwell's dream to lay waste Connaught
Galway renamed Gloucestergalway
        Yrland renamed Cromwellengland

Yrish hold 9% of their land 1660
                thanks to mister Crummy
        yr actions 'Regained'
        but 9/11 is 11/9 *Twin Towns*
                Drogheda-Dundalk
Slaughtered Cromwell Day
Puritans hack Glastonbury Hawthorn (Tor)
        and witch burnings (1664) to Somerset
                spells fate OC

Hic Jacit Diabolus Scimus

CLXIV

Milton thou should'st have been
           dug up, hung by yr remaining foetid hairs over

Thames-side spit, coated
           in dog turds, basted in urine & floating lice

           Lucifer lover, Satanist for yr
             leader, Crummy CromKiller
his favourite psalm 137 echoes his actions in County Louth
'happy shall he be, that taketh and dasheth thy children against the
storm'
& of course, Antonia Fraser, twenty-first century biographer
'must be accurate' she's 'Brit-hash' afterall:

'a great—if eternally controversial—man'
           Ah Cromwell, you were great killing—
            failed England not 'doing the'
            total genocide on Yrland

           & one thing Antonia, remember hubby 'Arold
            here he is cancelling out yr tome
(2002) Beckett's bicarbonate of soda friend, Harold
Pinter at Westminster Hall about Cromwell's
'Kill all the women and rape all the men'
'Excuse me General, shouldn't that be the other
way round?
and a nasty little whining loyalist voice
came forth
'the General knows what he is doing'

thus, they rape & kill clergy, men, women
  & children Drogheda/Drogheda

         (no poetry till now)
  & every summer school will mark it

         Cromwell like
Thatcher like Pais-Nazi-ley

         once in Yrland you
work for 'Regained'

unknowingly

hey, Antonia you've none of this
it would curldle yr Thames-side cream tea
      raspberry flan & pastry
 '3,000 including women and children
in the most cruel manner they could invent,
cutting off their members, and pieces of flesh,
which they wore in their hats triumphantly
two days after'
The Man in the Moon publication (1649)

no prisoners, 119 Catholic clergy including bishops, executed
near St Peter's (Drogheda)
genocide 20%
Yrish villages (thence) limited to no more
than 30 families by London decree

& dispossessed Yrish 'marched' to Connaught
forbidden to 'live' in Galway City
     forbidden, forbidden, forbidden […]
       to stutter […]

      & Plunkett's

severed head
St Peter's reliquary

parted lips 'Reg […]'

Carson Collins CANTOS

CLXXXII

out of the Shankill cradles rocking riot-culture to endgame GFA
kill-culture
look South 1.9.2.1.
Dublin Castle hands back after Yrish gunwork

how much graffiti rules this war:

thus far thou hast gone:
no orangeman has the right to fix a boundary
to the march o' Regained

'ALL our men should join the UVF'
—Carson circular letter 1913
this document hails 20th Century murders (Yrish)
pace: NOT for god and ulster
tit for tat
rat tat-tat-tat gunfire

typed-up, invented precedent
make a meal for Joseph Chamberlain's 1886 menu
'to Ulster a separate assembly'

Stormont bigot parliament for bigot people
Randolph Churchill & Bonar Law instigate
riots Belfast 'athwart' Gladstone's *Home Rule Bill* (1886)

1893 Second *Home Rule Bill*: 'shall not have home rule,'
spits Carson down his starched shirt front

Urbanity of Not-Never London's Knot
Duke of Abercorn, Thomas Sinclair
cost what it may, we will have nothing
to do with a Dublin parliament

Kipling bilges "Cleared" (1890) in rhyme
yes, Mr Eliot (Gt. Pt. otherwise)
        no land is waste according to London grabbers
                but Eliot yr bullshit, Kip imperialist
no responsibility, jingo Brit poet propagating political
programme—
Mr Eliot you quite requite him 'certainly not
aiming at
flattery of national, racial or imperial vanity, or attempting to
propagate a political programme […] much more an
awareness of responsibility'
this frikken London-nostalgic rhetoric Tommo Eliot-yuko
                Mr Kip racial reaper of Yrish murder
 'struth, fie foe, jolly rotten stuff old chap'
'They only took the Judas-gold from Fenians out of jail,
        They only fawned for dollars on the blood-dyed Clann-
na-Gael.
If black is black or white is white, in black and white it's down
They're only traitors to the Queen and rebels to the Crown'

                —R. K.
        off this bookshelf evermore F. U. R. K.

& Augusta Gregory to truckload of Brits outside Abbey,
                relates Lennox Robinson
            the olde lady shakes her brolley, shouts
                'Up the Webels!'

& Yrish-American gold dollars patronage for
'Regained'
'Ah-Mericay' they shout in Dublin town
out of the famine cradles endlessly rocking Diaspora
out of the phoenix coffin ships Diaspora
out of beán fíonn sí float the babes
of 'Regained'

CLXXXIII

& traditional Prod/Presby/Quake/Rep'licans null
                              homicidal orangey 'brethren'
                                    masonry of nailsmen
                                          no history root
dynasty of Prod/Presby Republicans
that Wolfe Tone (Protestant) foresaw
                    loathe the planted swamp slime bigots

break the connection with England [...]
source of all our political evils [...] *assert*
independence of MY country

& Lord Edward Fitzgerald Protestant
Robert Emmet, TCD drop-out Protestant
Joseph Biggar Presbyterian buys resting place for Henry Joy
McCracken Presbyterian
John Mitchel Presbyterian in print condemns orange order, evil
genociders
Thomas Davis Protestant poet cites lies of bigot Milton's
Eikonoklastes
Charles Stewart Parnell Protestant romantic
                    calls orangies *miserable gang who trade*
upon
                              name of religion
      & his royal confusion in 'adopted' greenness Archbish
Ussher Theology of Grail,
Ussher prays to wreck House of Westminster
upon any midnight dreary
      kill quaint kings Dunleary

& non-papists, non-catholics all: Henry Montgomery, Baron
Smith, Horace Plunkett
cannot support rigged hate-weapon to hold stolen land
and Casement (b. Dublin) denounced, defiled, degraded
Protestant Republican saint on right hand of Wolfe Tone
crucified upon Pentonville gallows
and Maud Gonne begat Republican prisoners' rights, beaten
                    by common law husband patriot, MacBride
who at firing squad
demands another cigarette delays squaddies their cup of scald
in Kilmainham, MacB faces British guns
            'go ahead shoot me […]'

1.9.1.6. Dublin defeats British Empire
crack-shot Constance 'Anglo' Markievicz 'Regained'
Douglas Hyde poet-translator *Presidente Republico Irlanda*
Hyde *outs* Ed Spenser *for* 'killings' for his prose against native-
names
            'they shall in time learne quite to forget the Irish
nation'

& Mr Shaw
& Mr Synge
& Willie Yeats 'turned' by Gonne by god
      green flowers, green with lust
Augusta Gregory (again), playwright, poet, theatre-lady
& O'Casey protestant-communist idolator of Connolly, Jas.,
& 'AE' George Russell on 1.9.1.6. 'Here's to you, Pearse
your dream not mine/But yet the thought for this you fell
turns all life's waters into wine'
and Beckett dramatic poet oppressed, afflicted, outcast
'vous êtes anglais, Monsieur Beckett?'
'Au contraire!' replies Sam with *Bushmills*

and signs *uptherepublic*

& Herr Francis Stuart says 'the Home Rule swindle'
means Westminster
(& despite loyaly cousins in Ballybogy) 'loves' Pearse,
Casement & Collins 'to
keep to true and lasting values
in the face of war hysteria & diversion of truth &
hypocrisy all around'

& Gerard Manley Hopkins S. J. favours Home Rule

'The soil of Yrland […] the people […]'—James Fintan Lalor,
1848
& Thomas Frances Meaghar's ancestor in HU
flicking archive access-cards
across the green baize 'Harvard in sight of Galway Bay'

there is no King's highway
in Portadown
nor thru Bagenal's Castle
nor in Lambeg
nor in Larne
nor Carrickfergus 'divorce cake castle'
& not never in Yrland's Shankill murder brood
not in Waterside
never on the slimed kill never britwalls of Derry
blood washed in green rain
& Sean Garland version (IRA's
somewhere over the Lagan-Foyle, way up high
Earl Hines & Monsieur Grappélli
chase blues to green

Irish Lullaby

a land you've heard of—not just once in an

&&&

where Troubles melt like lemon drops […]
that's where you'll find *beán fíonn sí*
birds fly over the Foyle and Lagan
why […] ?

'Regained'
London's paid loyalism bear impatience
beán fíonn sí demands 'Regained'

1171 onwards

cooks gelignite, burns houses, kills
until 'Yrland Regained'
(endgame of Yrish Republicanism)

CLXXXIV

Hell to thee C'arse Carson, '1912 Eddie'—
yes, HELL, don't misread it 'Hail'
oval face, demagogue mob mover
rivers of icy glass & blood
yr speeches Eddie

cohorts ride across the nightmare
fiery nostrils, sparks off
clanging armour, bullets repeat
until the chamber jams
AK47 clamps like a ceasefire
that does not last
c/f Winnie Churchill founder of Carsonism
to Gray July 1914: *i want peace by splitting*
the outstanding differences with Yrish acquiescence,
but if necessary over the head of both Yrish parties

Carson invents UVF in reprisal—
'any' career post-1912
'Regained' Part One arriving

quickie History (in 13 lines):
& *claritas*
Northern Ireland London (pron) 'Gnaw-Than, Eye-lawn'
failed never-democratic political entity created in London without
election or plebiscite under *Government of Ireland Act* (1920)
with support of planter unionist military lobby as state 'Majority' in
six of the nine north eastern counties, province of Ulster. Exclud-
ing three counties with Catholic/nationalist majorities: Donegal,

Cavan Monaghan and included Fermanagh and Tyrone with
nationalist minorities. Derry City and South Armagh/South Down
substantial Catholic/nationalist majorities re-zoned into electoral
populations 'deliberately' with voting restrictions/regulations so as
to *never* gain political status for Nationalists. Six Segregated
Occupied Counties of Yrland never approximates Democratic
principles as two-tier Police State rented by London incubating
sectarianism against Yrish.

                    & remains thus til 'Reg […]'

cartoon narrative + jokes

population dogs Carson's loyalies, County Donegal 1912
     16,000 sign his red blood parchment
         out of a possible 35,000
yet total Catholics is 140,000
population as Carson knows can never britify Ulster
            not 6 counties out of 9, not 32 out of 32

CLXXXV

'I find nothing in German history to compare with England's
treatment of Yrland'—Thomas Mann
                    good man Tomás, you'll have a double?
        Occupied Six counties is not 'Ulster' you lambeg plant-thugs

concludes today's history lesson
                                denied by Cromwellian bulldogs

perpetuates to 2019/20 [...] DUP's Foster 'Mrs Voster'
(correct spelling)
 & Maggie *Magna Carta* Thatcher parlour signee
of execution orders
                                        all this & more in War Epic
                banned in Downing Street, burnt in Fuckingham
Pally-ass
                        & when politicians choose
direct war to enliven procedural meetings,
elections & protocols

                Erich Maria Remarque in trenches WWI knows
                        Kaiser's weakness for war
                            'otherwise he would not become famous'
                        big corpse count, big reputation

death warmonger Churchill revels in it
                            something he enjoys since
leaden soldiers on starched linen cloths, his spacious bored
childhood attic—
privileged spoilt brat fantasies of WAR

                              on Eireann's green and
bloody shores, shored fantasies of drowning
              baby Churchill in his own shit

—shall not hold these graves

cut to *Ronnie Drews* bar, May Street, Belfast

bestride George's Market
1-minute pub-joke (strong language
& nudity)
Hallowe'en DUPP (Democratic Unionist Planters Party)
Frantic Dress Party Pigs
Ah, what to wear?

        ready to go balaclavas, real weapons
                as UDR, RUC, UDA, UVF, UFF, SAS—
uniforms available from orange halls
                stinking serge dyed oiled camouflage
                        state killing emblems
                trained by MI5/Brit Army
        Arlene demands Nigel Dodds 'go as'
                Batman, Peter Robinson *Spiderman*
                Jeffrey Donaldson *Robin* in green silks

& she 'Mrs Voster' as *Cat Woman* green
eye-shadow
Nigel draws London dole members room-key, goes off
with Mrs Voster, she in blonde wig, both
pissed, she strips
to her
                Orange knickers, he to his boxer shorts
                        with Paisley on the front

Carson on buttocks-side
'You've indulged in roast spit with
                two impotent dicks,' says Arlene
                'Drop yr knickers,' says Dodds
& she reveals a hairy sprayed tricolour

'I want to look like Michele O'Neill,'
                she flicks the blonde wig
'what d'you think?'
'I couldn't fuck a Fenian, Arlene, never
never never never.'
                'You prefer roast-spit with Paisley
                & Carson?'
                        'Aye,' says Dodds, 'I'd rather
be fucked up the ass by London.
King Billy Orange took it up the ass'.
'Don't let Teigs hear you,' says Voster Mörder Irisch

CLXXXVI

bounding parliamentary killers: Eddie Saunderson
comparison with any animal an insult
to all creatures great and small
If you ever try to enact it in Yrland we will crumble it to dust
'IT' being Home Rule thus Gladstone loses majority in
Westminster on HR Bill, bullied out of it by Thugs

Saunderson's castle in ruins by twentieth century

thus *Los Thug-os* hire another Eddie, Carson 'their' bum-Baron
to deliver

               in his starched shirt, treacle polished shoes,
stuffy three-piece suit
military pawn for London

               Kitchener disavows Carse as
Belfast blade-boy

                Kitch himself, initials HHK
a wildean with

               aide-de-camp 'secret' boyfriend
in armed forces, his Fitz—

            fucks him dressed in Union Jack nightshirt
into the icy Thames? Not quite—

Fitz and Kitch *en route* to Russia, diplomat-duo
June 1916
& as Uncle Epp shows it

            alliances form, break down, shift as tides—
                 entente, détente

intent, boundaries, peoples
                  allegiances each nationhood stubbornly
                  upon dead generations, fixed star sabre moon

                      back to Fitz & Kitch Kitchener—
plush cabin, comfy pillows 'n all
sunk off Orkney
both drowned while sucking lemons
when your country doesn't need you
                another London file stamped 'closed'
                  on the Ballylongford born boyo HHK
                    his Da retired army toff and
                      Kitchener born in County Kerry
                  You want the truth
You London can't handle the truth or have it printed

 war without weapons officially + these
weapons undercover
Larne Harbour: 19 April 1912, Fred Crawford & General
Hacket Pain (nomenclature)
                  negative karma names
                  England wars Yrland to 1998

CLXXXVII

YOU'! who never walked a trench '14-18'
you whose *Great War* slaughter is London's cannon fodder on
demand
                    you for whom Somme is mock-slogan
you never saw dying faces sinking in foreign mud
        for kinky Buskingham pugs
        wish to stiff Teigs in taxis (KAT 'kill all teigs')
                        fling them onto waste land
                    murder kill with more hate than any
        so called 'great war push' of Brit & Hun

            fooled for a crooked king, royal family feud
taught to march behind a band, earn a shilling, kill with bayonet
            cross-eyed in state homicide, stick it for perverted
king &
Kaiser, withered arm glued to his brazen baton
    who'd 'dressaged' in Jerusalem on a white horse
nephew of sunken bitter, queenly pudding faced fake-rhetoric
huntress

        of the widow gloom Tricky Vicky
left Kashmir as killing fields for Islam and Hindu—
england's crusades of death, dominion twixt Bann and Foyle
                    Lough Neagh sunset wears truth
wears war, promised ripple by ripple

                glad it's over, buried in 'triumph'

they who visit, designate undoing by their doing

close your eyes, see their doing, their 'wanhope' planting blame
bear with slaughter, dear bleeder
prick not fingers in yr ears, hear sounds of war
see red paint boiling
        in artist's studio, red sparks in the pot
metaphor for war, not decisive killing
battlefield bring Sassoon [ ] who spent early
        months 1918 in Limerick (of all places)
                Brooke (Rup'rd) establishment unlike
Owens (Wil'frd) got to by Sassanach
        Sassoon changes his poetry's politics to anti-London

                died a myriad of them also-rans WWII
every corner of every Yrish field
        that is for never England
                        find yr English heaven eastwards across
Yrish Sea
                east of Mona, east of Lands End, East of Stranraer

                Sassoon's rage to mental breakdown
                and actual

        you smug faced crowds with kindling eye
        who cheer when soldier lads march by
        sneak home and pray you'll never know
        the hell where youth and laughter go

                orangie halls pro 'what' patria

Sassy stuff, seen as sissy & 'too horrible' in 10 Downing Street
        when he shows poems to Edward Marsh (1916)
                far from trenches &
        rats, the nimble scavengers

Imperialism demands underclass, slums
breeding-ground grovelling
soldiers, glad of a chest full of bullets for a shilling

Granny you lie to Tennyson
nod off thru *In Memoriam*
yr favourite 'poems' are
'Collected Jingoism'

parades in pantomime, uniforms costumes
battle-virgin redcoats 'half-believed'
blood invisible in battle

never yr truth, learn it now, Yrish way—

CLXXXVIII

and beware 'Regained'
     more likely you'll get off scott free
         bums as usual
coasting clipped Nordy accents *isteach i Latharna*
Churchill's steel-bottomed *Clydevalley* 460 tons ship

'to place a motor-car at the disposal of the Provisional Govern-
ment [...]
should arrive at Larne on the night [...] very secret and important
[...]'—Bonar Law
Bonar Law & Order strictly for Propped-Up usshers of Six
Counties
     violence-stance, police state in making
a legally held weapon in the hand of every loyalist
26,000 rifles (minimum) 18,000 lodged in UVF depots
400-500 revolvers available, 2.5m rounds of ammunition

2.30 a. m. UVF dockers
grin unload loaded cargo, 'break' for tea-sandwiches
under lantern light, 'smoke if you have 'em'
but stay quiet
slimy Crawford's operational gun-runnings backed by London

how about a spot of narrative not fabula, 2 years later:

April 1914 another 20,000 rifles top-up, 2m more ammunition
Larne (tried & tested), Bangor & Donaghadee on board *SS Fanny*

loyalist fanny saying less than nothing
less still, corgi-bulldog class central London

absolute collusion: RIC did nothing to stop 'em
General Consensus
no Yrish millions to stop this
who will stop this, stop red & blue swathe paint
across map of north
steady stream licenses London gunrunners since 1172
1917 armaments UVF 55,000 weapons

to 80,000 weapons for Teig murders
(less distribution) for Monaghan, Cavan, Derry, Fermanagh
Teig majorities 'abominable' in these counties
'Carsonia' dream of ulster's nine counties held by force
Catholics you 'fucking taigs' venture out and get plugged
legally armed UVF
targets clearer than rainwater in a bucket
yr blood, our revenge
for being Yrish
for our failure to achieve our
Final Solution
yr impatient imperial failed centuries

CLXXXIX

nights of guns under moonlight, hands holding guns
what joy, the firing pin
            rifles against shoulders imagines a squirming Teig
               piles of Teigs piled high

Churchill, General Tudor, (Sir) James Craig-Murder
                  London's obeisance in titles, strewn about
                     sap lackeys who kiss royal arse
legally held arms UVF, Orange Policing
for the century up & beyond 2016
to dour sour counterfeit PSNI (police state northern Yrland)
original policy (as above) orangey policing, aye surely
       worth repeating like machine guns repeating
                     Simply the George Best
One Size Truncheon Cracks All Heads

Carson and Redmond on Whitehall's Chessboard

      hey Carson, Prime-Bigot-Primate
lost yr parliamentary seat in TCD, Dublin 'tried hurling'
               unionist past dead as the Republic rose
in the Land of Wild West Atlantic
Primate Eddie needs a constituency, moves black north, black

meaning
Hellfire Hate

not the subtle black colour
        of green Fenian faces in rebellion,
black-brothers North South East West
        and in Amerikay […]
                United Free Slates
                don't mention it in London town
        loads of fuckin Micks over there—
& conniving-Carson drums protestants to his identity
yet, Swift to Yeats to Casement are true Green
Carson needs cannon fodder promises; manic-career move
        see Carse' 1914 conscriptionist
                bodies being accounted
                        stock piled

        London's lackey recruiter

Killer Eddie finds a career
Biographers (HF!) Geoffrey Lewis, lie & lie & lie
 ignore the *Lusitania*, Carson's militarism
        UVF godfather license to kill
                civilian deaths keep the riot culture
                        riot mood, riots to imprint hate
sectarianism creed for a century
                of Carse for Hate in never-land 'Ulster'
                        educate for Hate
                                & to murder freely by law

Carson's 'Ulster' births the murder mind of loyalies

CXC

Asquith rages at mention of the Yrish Sea, damned headache
oversees fracas, token Buckingham
Palace (1914) Conference: segregate, split, divide, conquer

        would you believe merry Dublin
spews forth lank satanic spunk of bigotry
stony Carson, Dubliner dead on his Stormont statue
points to London, impotent finger
land border mentally writ before 1921 held by thumping flag wavers
                        dough-faces, shabby suits
                            sashes in blood orange sunset

            all empires fall from within
                UVF-Hell-Thug manifestations, Tudor Tory
Churchill's offspring
                Tory Thatcher's blood brother cousins

Churchie's bladeboy Carson & the Special
 Sectarian (SS) Constabulary
                    revenge for that damned Republic

'bloody harvest of Carsonism is being reaped
in Belfast. Race hatred, religious hatred, militarism,
rebellion have been preached there year after year […] the
gangs who organised the reign of terror are the very
people who protest [that] under even partial Home Rule,
be persecuted and denied religious liberty'
                        —*Daily Herald* 31 August 1920 (London)

arraign next witness, as if Westminster cares one orange flute

one Fenian corpse makes every difference to
their Final Solution that fails
since Strongbow bit off the first marriage
to 'a stinking native green bitch'

Asquith smells of perfume (like Disraeli)
& 'supposes' Carsonites
might exclude
Catholic parts of Down, Derry, Fermanagh
split Tyrone: it never happened.

Buckingham Palace Conference (1914)
Sham George V (they come in Vs)
George Five warns Civil War, withdraws […]
Carson longs for All Ulster, All Ireland Union
Craig pushes his luck to Six Counties of Nine
holds veto on everything, crooked elections
politics: overclass underclass culture

Gen. Mkl Collins clear-eyed on Yrish Question
'there is no Irish Question'
'unity of Ireland is going to be my main idea'
'give us back our country' & thereafter stops
asking, both guns cocked

bullets in pockets, in
luggage, hence heavy overcoat

26 out of 32 ain't bad, bad for 1921
rooftop to rooftop
bullets
legends & facts, print both

CXCI

—and Ó Rathaille cursed them (1703)
hundred years before they hung, quartered
Emmet (aged 20) TCD student revolutionary
sweet blood of youth, Emmet's executioner holds the head up
warning James Street
unruly populous

                       & for this alone 'Regained'

                       O London green murders

                       'a wave of criminal lust rose and
possesses England,

                       there is a reign of terror, under a set
of indecent bullies

                       like Bottomley of *John Bull*, and the
other bottom-dog

                       members of the House of Commons
[…] *Tuatha De*

                       Danaan! Be with me. Be with me.'

Lawrence (D. H.) *Kangaroo*
                       (yea, Lawrence *Danaans*
ancient name for Greacians)
thou shalt not kill us England, Emmet gives the hangman
a lesson on how to tie a knot, converses with
presiding clerics before mounting the scaffold
shall never kill us, centuries of chances

& they swing Kevin Barry (aged 18) UCD student a hundred
years
beyond
Barry takes a few with him until his gun jams

& Dublin will wipe the streets in Brit anaemic blood
One Nine One Six—week's warm up for
War of Independence

Barry's sister 'dies' too, lives on afflicted
he'd braved it, their last meeting about Shaw's theatre play
they'd seen the character Dick Dudgeon
                who was spared the drop

'Twin Gun' Collins wants to spring Barry
& Peadar Clancy, Dick McKee & Conor Clune
tortured shot 'trying to escape' from Dublin Castle
Collins hits the Cairo Gang Intelligence Unit
 Toff Brits shot in one morning, Collins lowers his Guinness
breakfast
'my conscience is clear
[…] I pay them back in their own coin'

Gen. Tom Barry IRA Kilmichael ambush
thus, Henry Joy (McCracken) co-founder of
United Irishmen has a Hit Squad
                                defiance quietens London
                                    'in their own coin'

Africa South, your destiny slugs it to them who swings so many

the war dogs snarl in suits de Klerk, Vorster, Botha
                swing Solomon Mahlangu (22) in Pretoria

crooked evidence on the ANC volunteer, choked
on their twisted rope breaks his neck for freedom
                              slashes Africaans blood grip

& Seán de Brún *The Oak*, Derry re-aligns three boxed darts
tilts the Bulmers pint-glass—

                              'body bags for Brits […]'
Collins 'on little sleep'
back-bar Wynns yawns on a binge, Stout bottles
                              American handguns,
chambers studded in
bullets, cigarettes alight in the dark, tells his Squad
Dick McKee & Mick McDonnell
lads, always two guns […] head shots
[...] shakes his head before he drinks
('The Collins-Squad' increases beyond 20 in 1920)
              & hubris Gen. Collins richochet
                    to the head, Béal na mBláth
                         late Summer
       "inside job" you better believe it, "inside job"
                 richochet from grassy knoll
—does this sound like a bunch of coincidences?
              aged 31 'mouth of flowers' kisses beán fíonn sí
                    mouth of blossoms, mouth of green
                         'Regained'

CXCII

'Collins is a corner-boy in excelsis' spake
Cromwell Churchill
slobbers cigar bile from teeth
London's two-legged foetid Hippo
'and as for de Valera [...]'
hatred keeps war on the boil
general demarcation for Yrish wars

dust down ye olde blueprint
rules of engagement
killings, arrests, surveillance
house searches, knocking softly on the
door of course, in case
you terrify children, doing the usual killing
greening up the phoenixes

So—or thus it came to pass, as it
was in the beginning
forgotten by London not along river banks
mountain tops, tree tops, villages and towns
across green sea in green land
Carson equipped 'his' local electorate covert army
plants population upon the natives

Carson's sidekicks: George Richardson & R.W. Wallace—
Wallace demands
'[from] the present time on (1913) Sir Edward wants it all loyal,
all members UVF'

war-men hold half a dozen counties to ransom
via Churchill's UVF
who arms them & Carson sucks Winston's tits
for his parliamentary seat in England
& Granny Vicky's cannon fodder
      Granny carcase
Granny's war, remember 1914-18
royal feud creates trenches & battlefields
                    commemorations for Royals
      keeping diaries, keeping awake (if possible)
                    watching parades
meanwhile fat Granny frowsy black silk
presumes Yrland free
                    for fodder, mounds of fresh-flesh for wars
                    relentless catalogue of gunfire rhythm
                        four years in France & Belgium
                        daily thunder artillery & guns
                              daily rattle printing presses
                              rhetoric of machine gun fire
                              ink-wrappings propaganda
                              nausea newspapers amidst
                              tobacco stained fingers
                      lice under fingernails, rum stink
corned beef slime across stale bread,
engine oil tea

burial duty, time off

CXCIII

and Carson rigs *Lusitania Inquest*
forces Captain 'Bowling Bill' Turner to lie

Oscar Wilde pursues libel, pilloried gaoled
by Carson's guile London's hypocrisy
Wilde 'British playwright'
                              born in Dublin

& Wilde lectured in Derry (1884)
crosses Foyle, shivers in a silk shirt
Yrish greatest talkers since Greeks
                              and does the orgasm
        joke 'Niagara Falls first disappointment
in American marriage'

his lines inherit Jane Elgee's Fenianism
into *Reading Gaol, The Ballad of*
                              Oxford knee breechers hung up for
Victorian Gaol garb
                              poet enters hard core politics

'for only blood can wipe out blood
        and only tears can heal'

first disappointment in orangey-marriages:
Irish Republic shoots into being 1916-1921—
                London hates Uncle Sam
                        adopting
yob faced 'English language thieving' rabble

blarney drunken hooligans
dirty wide-eyed gap-toothed peasants Teigs

orange orgasm stalled
by 'famous' Anglo-Irish Treaty
'Ulster Covenant' local cabal

& Fitzgerald eggs Thatcher 1985
backed by Capitol Hill's iron shamrock
Yrland boils orangie paranoia
to puce pink fever colour

orange orgasm only possible through catholic murders
England's private lies/public lies

'One torpedo sunk the *Lusitania*' Captain Turner says in Yrish
Inquest
'Two torpedoes sunk the *Lusitania*' Turner replies in
 Carson's 'Official' Inquest—
science steers history to one torpedo
Turner recants in old age 'One torpedo!'
lies print 'true' in London
America calls up armies 1915 for Europe
avenge drowned *hoi polloi*
London's green nightmares
includes 1.9.1.6.
'they lost Yrland!'
London Admiralty keep *Lusitania* on a slow course
did it matter how many torps [...]
elementary my dear Winston, ONE torpedo
doesn't matter
propaganda WWI matters

London draws (American) Wilson into Granny's War
        Uncle Epp's *old bitch gone in the teeth* is Victoria
          living augur of death of Empire

and Carson works for landlords during 'Irish' Land Wars
secures 'partition of sects, from one footstalk of right'
          O blimey, those fucking Yrish what
can we do with them
          eradicate them, their 'Swineglish'
        hateful, gloomy mopes swilling whiskey
          lick it off a kitchen sink, cow's leg,
toilet floor they would
          KAT (Karson-Anti-Teig)

CXCIV

O aye, and who not sick by his detritus
slime on sea green, moss green
polished laurel leaf & the emerald eyes of beán fíonn sí

so & thus, *encore* Carson speaks
'Bill for the Better Governing of Yrland' (1920)
Southwards towards Dublin-Mexico *The Partition Bill*
meaningless oath of allegiance to king Georgie
grey hairs and successors according to law, *so help me Gad*
'If we were saddled with Donegal, Cavan and Monaghan...will bring in
an additional 260,000 Roman Catholics. The figures will at once show
where the difficulty comes in. We have to refer in these matters to
Protestant and Catholic [...] because these are really the burning questions
over there. We should like to have the very largest area possible, naturally.'
C'arse means staunch bigot orange-prods burn out Catholics
        graffiti: *London's eunuch-orangey minions*
   musty suits, pastry faces, orange paint caked on
army boots
      largest possible prod-majority police
Churchill's weapons
       police state for a protestant people
        &
       London lies, back to narrative:

(Sir shit) Henry Wilson prepares 'accommodations' for loyalist
refugees

indemnity charity fund £1m: *für die* disabled, widows and orphans

as in Hamburg (August 1913) Carson meets Kaiser
incestuous stink Kaiser Bill, Killer Bill II
first cousin of Georgie V
grandchild of sniffy Vicky, aka Granny Murder

Killer Bill II promises army 'if Home Rule is forced
on the protestants of Yrland'
hence Kaiser loyalist

remember, ah you do
done by an Act of Parliament in Westminster
for loyalist fodder (if capitalised here, read 'error')
loyalists rigged majority (for a while)
nationalist underdogs 'Do Not Bark'
pace: simple cartoon force-politics
& that Carson with Hamar Greenwood (secretary hammer)
calls Michael Collins 'head of the murder gang'
and like Sir Henry Wilson (British State killer) 'not to deal'
with 'Rebels'
no never no more, for they play the Wild Rovers

thus (28 September 1912) mob declaration
similar to fealty for Henry VIII's declaration 'King of Yrland'
(1541)
        place he never set foot in, except his mounted horse & foot
Earl of Ormond translates Henry's new title into Gaelic
for all present makes him proxy linguistic kink (not misspelt)

in Dublin parliament, read this as
partitioning all Ysland by London

 let's break for lunch, you know yr history
        repetition to those who know
the tunes […] democracy a melody
        lyricists at large, meanings replete
firgureheads, despots will nilly control the mob in actions

call it politely 'Ulster Covenant of Sectarian Throat Slashers'
'whatever the consequences' signing principle
& Kipling's 'Ulster 1912' published in Tory *Morning Post*
not *The Times* who half-support Home Rule
want out of Yrland lick, lock, stock and gun-barrel
                              we know the war prepared
                              on every peaceful home,
                              we know the hells declared
                              for such as serve not Rome
                                        —R. K.

work it up Kipling, turn flood-gates of riot to 'Open'

lies, lies, lies loyalist bigotry, hate & threat
'How loyal hearts should kneel
To England's oldest foe'
                        not admitted by London this indelible
planted planter Symphony of Incensed Hatred

                        incredible backward compliment

                Kipling rhymer extraordinaire gave a son to
                        the 1914-18 bloodbath,

changes his politics
                        son as corpse for king, country and glory
                                and O the change in him
humans in grief change
more than seasons

more than faces

                            this basted this, this basted
in grief, otherwise
                            no ballast dull beat of grief
                                killing present time
featureless fruitless
                                but for 'Regained'
that grief shall find there deep green recompense

CXCV

just to 'kneecap' (misprint 'recap') for those taking
'History Major':

you know Kipling, Yrland is England's oldest foe
has supporters Lord Rothschild as fairy (PC?) Disraeli before,
hear it Sirrah, Edward Elgar's 'Pomp and Circumstance'
    martial music for Saxon hordes at slaughter

history easier than making bread:
    find the graves, follow the money, follow land grabbers,
        follow innocents slaughtered and victors
            lie-ing up for their gold fillings
        and visit Westminster by stinky Thames

Mr Kip donates, not only ranting poem (above)
but £30,000 to the killers
AND pays full in grief, son John
irony of ironies: Lieutenant in Yrish Guards
face blown off by one of Kaiser's shells
that is loyalism to Granny Victoria and bombshells from grandson
    Kaiser for Kip's son, son of a kip
    & 'in the face' popular feature of 35 Year's War
   loyalist methodology: shoot point blank into faces
 Fran O'Toole (1975) Miriam Daly (1980)
John Finucane (1989) Rosemary Nelson (1999)
'—more,' yells London, 'we'll pay for more lager'
June 1915 UVF cruel face shots
    words cruel, history lies, cruelty as propaganda
        war lying active propaganda

                war consumes corpse flesh, insatiate
            tell us something newer than old wars

so back in 1914 (blah de blah) Westminster plays 2 sets of Volun-
teers
                       backing two horse Irish Derby
                          winner decided but
                                   ultimate winner foreseen
              hence IRA (1983) Shergar kidnap (global pub joke)

                   weighted accordingly, slowly over century
            push towards planters and two-horse race
                           fakery pakery London pride
               who did the shooting, who died?
Yrish and Ulster, both varieties cannon fodder in France
& Belgium, regimental insignia (barely) recognisable on some
war dead—
thus Asquith August 22, 1914
'Yrish on both sides are giving me
lot of trouble [...] submerge whole lot of them and their Ysland
for, say, ten years under waves of Atlantic'
poor Asquith with war on his banquet menu—
Home Rule off menu

1916 Irish-American opinion: US still not in War
Lloyd George goes Unionist to any/every *Unionista*
'at the end of the provisional government period Ulster does not,
whether she wills it or not, merge with the rest of Yrland'
The Government of Ireland Act
piece of blood stained paper, blood stained ink
      on fidget hands
typed in Westminster, breakfast & cigars
              no treaties without cigar-smoke
              peace pipes farce is future 35 year war

CXCVI

addenda for any patriots in the house:

December 1916 ensure Ulster fodder, Lloyd George 'elevates'
Carson, First Lord of Admiralty: 'my only qualification
for being head of Navy is I am very much at sea'
$$\text{Carson's line in comedy}$$

power manacles power on full power

no sooner First Lord than everyone wants him ousted
& Carson shock when Treaty signed with
Gen. Collins & 'nasty' Dublin rebels
getting *Anglo-Irish Treaty*
     London version to split Yrland
          seed Civil War for Natives
     plant 35 Years War for 1960s, 70s, 80s, 90s

    Mr Thug C'arse Carson seethes, rails at London's fickle loyalty
                anyone out there west of the Isle of Mann—
had known, always knew 'I was only a puppet, and
so Ulster, so Yrland, political game
get Conservatives back into power'

       repeating cartoon history
Mrs Voster DUP, 2017-19-20
              keep & get Tories back, keep Tories in power

and finally, old fruit C'arse admits (by letter) to Sir John Marriott
6 November 1933 'the elements that had real power

were not only anti-English but really far from civilised
my long experience of government of the country,
I have always felt parties of disorder would in
long run come to the top. I quite agree
in the end a question of nationhood'
Good man C'arse at least you admit bigotry, British Question
            & Final Solution—
Green Final Solution if America will back it
        London kneels on green carpet under Yrish axe
                kissing Yrish snakes
                        & Banks that bankroll the Ysland
                England says 'sink orange scums
                                in Teigland'

'Celts have done nothing in Yrland but create trouble, disorder.
Yrishmen who have turned out successful are not in any case I
know,
of true Celtic origin...' Arse C'arse knoweth all—

                    ah sure Eddie, you went with it
                        scary sectarian bordered off 6
                            reaps rapes carcase fruits
                        Churchill's blood, sweat and tears
                        'torture chambers' & 'collusions'
                        drawing room downing street mode
                            war-horrors surge it towards
                                    'Regained'

CXCVII

puke inducing, plain rank disgusting
abattoir summery day
there you have it
there be more, abominable Carse
un-royal wanna be royal arse

fee-fie-fo-fum comes to pass breeds division + goode 35 years
war
& Leonard Stanford Merrifield statue
undraped stone corpse July 8, 1933
ready for scum-drum day
before Stormont & they bury the auld cunt
in St Anne's Cathedral
non-fake tyrant, stir in plenty slaughter with his coffee—
    final recap:

'Reinforce Ulster as much as she wants' (Churchill, February
1922)
mid-1922, Henry Wilson increases garrison
5,500 A Specials
19,000 B Specials
plus undisclosed number C Specials
straight-sectarian-line, note Somme
claims 'exorb' casualties for loyalists BUT
more Catholic-Yrish die in WWI:
210, 000 enlist from 32 County Yrland
round dead-figures 28,000
15,000 returned to 'Black North'
join Ulster Special anti-Teig Constabulary

note Southern Irish regiments
Gallipoli, all Dublin Fusiliers

France and Belgium the Nationalist Yrish fight
            for London:
'Royal' Dublin Fusiliers
The 'Royal' Irish
The Connaught Rangers
The Munster Fusiliers
Redmond's National Volunteers
        (GBS's *O'Flaherty VC* pro-Brit jingo)

                            war policy seeps
                            slow deliberate drip killing
                    Yrish deaths London demands
            case proven, bigotry borders Six primed
        by London, Carson puppet with orange hand
                            shoved up his backbone
                    bucket of mouth, sour-milk hate

He did. Royalists-Loyalists East of Bann on beermat myths
fist red-hands pour real blood: no siege in Derry
Boyne not decisive (weather, flooding)
orangey Dutch sashes = putrefaction corpses
play without melody, tinny flutes dying ducks
doom-march poker faces, plod pantomime bands

'We are also worried about Yrland' Churchill to Roosevelt June
13, 1940

                            loyalism primes division
                    6 counties, corpse blue 'dilly dally'

corpse red 'shilly shally'

        regimental London brutes
        untrue history, pseudo-Carson

Belfast forced red/blue
stained clothes

        police state, planter policed elections
        rigged electorate zones, hold majority
        (Calhoun's concurrent majority not

read into Six Counties)

        employment rigged towards loyalists
        two-tier society: Teig-proles

Orwell's *Ulster 1984*

        Big Brother London bum Brother
        loyalist bed & b'fast (Belfast)
        loyalist identity *falsetto con troppo*

dole profile/non job profile

free loaders' handouts

        no-land mob know nothings, no-history
        Six Counties Orwell's *1921*

        definitive reading *1984*
            supports 'Regained'

O'Brien 'Paddywhack name'
        Winston interrogation, awaits execution
in Room 101
        read 10 Downing Street for Room 101
where rats consume
        Winston Churchill
        Orwell's *Ireland 2084*

                        does that seem like a bunch of
coincidences or what—?

                                    not for one minute &
                                    solid citizen Eric Blair, never
Tony Blair

                        Edinburgh University Press (2007)
Ian Wood *Crimes of Loyalty*

                        UK propaganda to hold the Six
                Antrim's SS barracks green corrugated
fence graffito: **KAT (2020)**

                                    case proven